# Literary Criticism
## A Handbook for Beginners

Blessed E. Ngoe

ISBN: 9781704749723

# DEDICATION

In memory of Gerald

# CONTENTS

# ACKNOWLEDGMENTS

All authors whose works were consulted to produce this volume. Professors and Lecturers of the Department of English, University of Buea, especially Emeritus Professor Kashim I. Tala, Professor Nol Alembong, Professor Charles N. Teke, Professor Ann Tanyi-Tang of blessed memory, Chief Dr. Ngeh A. Tata, Dr. Nekang née Frida Mbunda, Dr. Kelvin Ngong Toh, Dr. Eunice Fombele, Dr. Emmanuel Njume, Mrs Doreen Mekunda and Mr. Epey Andrew B. for introducing me to the world of literature.

I am also indebted to the following for their massive support in various ways in the course of putting this work together: Messrs. Akem Henry, Rodrick Lando, Nseme Stephen, Mbain Derek, Isidore Abah, Levis Ngoe, Kelvin Moriya, Didan Ngoe, and Isifu Wirfengla; Mme. Langue A. Patricia and Mme. Alfreda Ngoe; Ms. Enanga Numa, Ms. Felicita Ngoe, Ms. Elsie Wase and Ms. Perpetua Ngoe.

# FOREWORD

The teaching/learning of literature in English has been and remains a challenging and an arduous task both to native and non-native speakers of the English language. So far, one of the reasons advanced to explain this phenomenon is the ever-evolving nature of the English language itself. This implies that in order to appreciate literary texts in their wider intellectual and historical contexts, one needs to have a sophisticated mastery of the language.

However, the good news here is that without claiming to have a perfect grasp of the English language, the author of this book has painstakingly made the task an easy one both for teachers and learners. Consequently, this book comes to serve as an aide to both students and teachers, especially those whose language of instruction is or will be English, but who have had a very distant relationship with the language.

Also, while this handbook cannot claim to have exhausted all that needs to be known as far as the tools of literary criticism are concerned, it has nevertheless taken into consideration, the immediate needs of students. In essence, it is a working manual for beginners in literary studies as it provides brief definitions and descriptions of a variety of literary terms which are invaluable to any serious budding literary scholar.

The book will be beneficial to students of secondary and post-secondary levels, especially those who intend to pursue literary criticism as an academic career. There are more than one hundred terms and concepts briefly defined with incisive examples and illustrations provided to furnish readers with the best that is expected of them at their early stage in literary criticism.

Roderick Lando

M.A (Eng.), University of Buea

Lecturer, CUIB, Buea

# THE LANGUAGE OF LITERARY CRITICISM

**To the Reader**

You are about to enter into the world of literary expression. As you go through the pages of this book, you will find that the author has simplified your search by assigning the entries here in alphabetical order. We could have assigned the entries according to subjects. For example, we could have had sections dealing particularly with the various literary genres (Poetry, Prose and Drama) or sections dealing with style, sound devices or figurative language. That approach would have been very rewarding too. However, the author deemed it worthy to introduce you to the worthwhile task of sorting out the classes under which the entries discussed in this book exist. This way, your critical abilities will be spurred; hence, your grasp of literary criticism will also speed up.

It should be noted that the terms you find here are like tools with which you build your critical perception in literature. They constitute the nerves of literary criticism and not the whole itself. To be able to launch full critical potency in literature is to understand how effectively these terms work together in giving a literary piece its full definition. Literary creators sometimes make use of these terms unconsciously. It is the place of the critic therefore to identify them and relate them effectively to the message that the literary piece sets out to convey.

As a critic, you are therefore required to command a mastery of most, if not all, of the terms here defined to help you translate the thoughts of the literary creator to his/her audience effectively.

It is true that some of the terms here may not relate directly to your immediate literary space, especially when we consider culture and other social parameters as determinants of literature. The Haiku, for example, may appear to be out of place to the Cameroonian (or African) literary pupil, but its particular features may not be totally divorced from the general features that go with poetry. Hence, even outside the precincts of one's literary space, the pupil must find it worthwhile to understand the workings of particular literary cultures so as to equip himself/herself with what it takes to face the general or universal literary sphere.

Blessed E. Wa-Ngoe
Buea, 2016

# A

## Abstraction, language of

This refers to the use of words that communicate ideas or insubstantial realities, instead of to exact or tangible matter or realities. Many people think that *beauty* is a thing of *the past* and that the *joy* of *art* has gone awry.

## Act

An act is a major unit of a play or drama. Some African dramatists don't care much about dividing their plays into *acts*.

## Allegory

This refers to narrative work of art or drama in which the elements (characters, settings and plot) are meant to convey a moral lesson. To accomplish this, things, settings and persons are often used as symbols that represent certain values or realities in life. Ernest Hemingway's novel, *The Old Man and the Sea*, is often regarded as an allegory of man's struggles with human and non-human elements in life.

## Alliteration

This is the repetition of consonant sounds at the beginning of words in poetry or speech. For example

*The devil dealt a deadly deed when I couldn't deny Christ*

## Allusion

This is the literary technique in which the writer or speaker refers to a character, place, situation, or idea from some other discipline, time, or work of art. Usually, allusions are drawn from history (historical allusions), the Bible (biblical allusion) or from nature (allusion to nature). Robert Bolt alludes to history in his play, A *Man for all Seasons*.

## Ambiguity

Language is said to be ambiguous when it expresses more than one meaning in a single term or passage. In the conventional usage of language, ambiguity is a mark of poor command. In literature however, the splendor of language is in its quality to suggest various sheets of connotation.

## Analogy

We use analogy when we compare things which are otherwise different to show how similar they are. Analogy can help us explain unfamiliar or unknown things by comparing them to familiar ones. In Plato's *Allegory of the Cave*, the unfamiliar phenomenon of the World of Forms and of the World of Realities is compared to people in a cave.

## Antagonist

An antagonist is a person, a force or a phenomenon in a story or drama that opposes the main character or protagonist. In Hemingway's *The Old Man and the Sea*, the sharks are the antagonist.

## Aphorism

An aphorism is a short, sharp statement that expresses a wise or clever observation about human experience. For example, the expression, *Life is a battle* is an aphorism that relates to the struggles that one must endure while living.

## Apostrophe

In this figure of speech, the speaker addresses an inanimate object, an idea, or an absent person or even a corpse. Most incantations, prayers and invocations are apostrophes.

## Aside

Usually in a play, an aside is a comment, made by a character, which is heard by the audience but is not heard by other characters on stage. Shakespeare's Twelfth Night makes use of asides. The aside is meant to reveal a character's thoughts.

## Assonance

This refers to the repetition of similar vowel sounds, especially in verse. In the following line, the /ai/ sound is repeated.

I see my wife like all I like.

## Atmosphere

The prevailing mood or feeling put across by a piece of writing. Mood can be sad, suspenseful, joyous, passionate etc.

## Autobiography

This refers to the story of someone's life, written by that person. The book, *Audacity of Hope* is Barack Obama's autobiography.

# B&C

## Ballad

A ballad is a poem or song that tells a story. Formerly known as **Folk Ballads**, these forms of art were originally passed down orally from generation to generation before being written down.  Today, literary ballads are written in the style of folk ballads.

## Blanc verse

This refers to poetry which is written in unrhymed iambic pentameter. An iambic pentameter consists of lines which have five pairs of syllables each, with each of the pairs made up of an unstressed syllable followed by a stressed syllable. The following verse is in iambic pentameter.

*Then my fee buried, I to them returned*

## Caesura

This refers to a pause in a line of poetry to draw attention to a word or to produce rhythm. The following verse has caesuras in it.

*The night was long, the sleep was short, but she lay young and tall.*

The caesuras here occur after *long* and *short*.

## Catalogue (catalog)

This is when a writer lists images, people, ideas, details or events in their literary piece.

## Character

A character is an individual in a literary work. Characters are either **main** or **minor**. The main character plays a central role in the story with his/her/its full personality qualities coming forth in the story. A minor character plays a minimal role and is used only to develop the plot of the work where necessary. Characters can further be classified as **round, flat, stereotype, dynamic** or **static**. A round character displays an array of behaviors which may sometimes be contradictory. A flat character reveals only one personality trait throughout the work of art. When a character is typically flat, it is said that the character is stereotype or stock (meaning that such a character is very familiar and could be boring). Such a character could also be called static. A dynamic character changes and grows in the course of the story.

## Characterisation

This refers to the method an author uses to reveal the individuality traits of their characters. Characterization is either **direct** or **indirect**. In direct characterization, the author comments explicitly on the individual. In indirect characterization, the character traits of an individual are revealed through what they say or do and through what others say and think about them.

## Classicism

Classicism refers to a style of art that reflects the principles and values of ancient Greece and Rome. The style of classical works is usually pure in form, harmonious and simple. William Shakespeare's *Julius Caesar* and *Antony and Cleopatra* are classical works.

## Cliché

A word or phrase becomes a cliché when it has been used over and over again by the same writer in the same work of literature or in other works. One of Shakespeare's best-known clichés is the statement; *something is rotten in the state of Denmark.*

## Climax

In a narrative, climax refers to the point of greatest emotional intensity and involvement. Climax is usually attained immediately before the point of resolution or when the story or play is taking a new turn to resolve a conflict.

## Comedy

Comedy refers to a humorous type of drama that often ends happily. William Shakespeare's *Twelfth Night* is a comedy.

## Comic relief

This is when a humorous episode is inserted into a serious drama so as to break the anxiety and yet underscore the seriousness of the story.

## Conceit

It refers to a detailed and extended metaphor that dominates a part of a piece of writing or an entire poem. Customarily, the conceit compares a natural phenomenon or an everyday life happening to the subject or theme of the poem or passage.

## Concrete language

This is opposed to abstraction and is the use of clear rather abstract or ideological concepts in communicating issues in a work of art. Specific words for tangible phenomena are used rather than words relating to values. Words such as pan, boy, sheep, the sea, telephone etc. are concrete while words such as love, mystery, hate, etc. are abstract.

## Confessional poetry

This is a movement which began in the 1950s in which writers in poetry handled issues relating to their personal experiences. Some of the otherwise shameful aspects of human conduct like drug abuse and sexual disorientation were described directly in poetry by those who actually perpetuated them. Some of the prominent poets of this movement include Robert Bowell and Sylvia Plath.

## Conflict

Conflict in literature refers to the struggle that a writer establishes between two opposing characters, forces or phenomena in drama or prose. Conflict is either internal or external. Internal poetry occurs when a character witnesses strife between two opposing thoughts or desires in their mind. External conflict on its part is the struggle that exists between a character and some outside force. This could either be another character, a force of nature, destiny, or society.

## Connotation

Connotation refers to the meaning suggested by a word in relation to the context and not to its dictionary definition. It is sometimes called the deeper meaning. Its opposite is denotation which is the direct or shallow meaning given to a word- its literary meaning. A words connotation can be positive, negative or neutral.

## Consonance

This refers to the repetition of similar consonant sounds especially within or at the end of words. In the following line the [ch] sound is repeated at the end and within the verse.

*Teach them to clutch upon the mantle of the church*

## Couplet

These are two uninterrupted, corresponding lines of poetry which usually rhyme and form a stanza.

*O fairy land, the land of birth*

*That which stands firm o'er the face of the earth*

## Crisis

The crisis in a story or drama is the moment of high anxiety or tension, in which a decision is required to attain a solution.

# D

## Denotation

See Connotation

## Denouement

This refers, in a narrative, to the conclusion or resolution of the plot.

## Dialect

This is a variation of a language spoken by a particular group of people often from a particular region and time. Slight differences in pronunciation, vocabulary and grammar occur between dialects and the standard form of a language. Londo and Lolue are both dialects of Oroko. Oroko, Duala and Mokpe can be considered dialects of a proto-Sawa Bantu language.

## Dialogue

Dialogue in a narrative and drama refers to the conversation between characters. African novelists make use of very little dialogue in their stories.

## Diction

This refers to a writer's choice of words. Diction helps the reader understand the writer's voice and style. Diction can also help readers understand a writer's mood and attitude towards the subject matter. A skilled writer therefore chooses his words very carefully to put across a particular tenor and implication

## Drama

Drama refers to a story which is intended to be acted or performed on stage by actors. A drama script has the following elements; **stage directions** (which explain how actors should look, dress or talk), **dialogue** (which is the conversation between characters in the drama), **acts** (which are the parts into which the drama has been divided (acts may also be split into **scenes**), and there are specifications for lighting, setting and scenery, stage props and sound effects.

## Dramatic monologue

A dramatic monologue is a form of dramatic poem in which the speaker directs a speech to a silent listener.

## Dramatic poetry

This refers to poems with characters which are revealed through dialogue and monologue. In this kind of poetry characters are also revealed through description.

# E

## Elegy

An elegy is a poem that mourns the death of someone or that regrets another great loss.

## Enjambment

This, in poetry, refers to the continuation of a sentence across a line break without a punctuated pause between lines. The following lines are enjambed:

*Names have been upon my lips, but none has been so sweet*

*To make my senses free for once and think but only love*

## Epic

An epic is a long narrative poem that tells of the adventures of a hero. Epics reflect the values of the society of their origin by interlacing myth, legend and history. The epic of Sonjara or Sondiata (Sonjata) is one of Africa's most important epics.

## Epigram

This is a short poem which expresses a lot of wisdom. It is usually a saying. The poem 'Beauties' by B. E wa Ngoe is an epigram.

## Epiphany

It refers to a sudden intuition that makes a character realize the meaning or essence of something.

## Epithet

An epithet is a nickname, a phrase or an adjective used in the narration of epics to identify or describe a recurring character, place, object or event. For example, in *The Epic of Sonjara* narrated by Fadigi Sosòkò and recorded by William Johnson, the hero, Sonjara is called, "Simboin, Lion born of cat".

## Essay

This is a short piece of non-fiction writing on any given topic. An essay communicates an idea or an opinion. Essays are either formal or informal. The formal essay is usually serious and impersonal while the informal essay blends information, entertainment and discussion together. Another form of essay is the personal essay which is a kind of informal essays that makes use of personal references. Jean Paul Sartre's "Existentialism is a Humanism" is an example of a formal essay.

## Exemplum

An exemplum as the name suggests is a short story that demonstrates a moral lesson by serving as an example.

## Exposition

This is the part of the plot line in a novel, a story or other narrative that introduces the characters, the setting and the situation.

## Expository Writing

This is a kind of writing that informs and explains. It is also called an exposition and is usually written as prose.

**Extended Metaphor**

An extended metaphor compares two unlike things in various ways throughout a paragraph, a stanza or an entire literary piece.

# F&G

## Fable

A fable is a short story with a simple plot that usually uses animal characters to communicate a moral lesson.

## Falling Action

In a narrative, this refers to the action that comes immediately after the climax.

## Farce

This is a type of comedy with fantastic, ridiculous characters, situations or events. Oscar Wild's *The Importance of Being Ernest* is often considered a farce.

## Fiction

This refers to a narrative whose characters and situations are not real but are inventions of the writer. However, some aspects or elements of some fictional works may have real life situations or experiences as their springboards. Short stories, novels, dramas and some narrative or dramatic poems are fictional works.

## Figurative Language

This is language used for descriptive effect, in order to convey ideas or emotions (Glencoe Literature, 2000: R6). The literal truth is not found in figurative language. Rather, this kind of language goes beyond the literal dimension of language to convey special meaning. Figurative language is most prominent in poetry and Elizabethan drama. Metaphor, irony, personification, symbolism and simile are all figurative language.

## Flashback

Flashback is a technique in literature during which there is an interruption in the chronological order of a narrative (and even drama) to show an earlier event or situation. Flashback helps readers understand the background to certain occurrences in a story as it unfolds. In Linus T Asong's *No Way to Die*, Dennis engages in flashbacks to tell of his past academic achievements and of his relationship with Dr. Max.

## Flash-forward

This is the direct opposite of flashback which is the interruption of the chronological sequence of a narrative to leap forward in time.

## Folklore

Folklore embodies the traditional beliefs, customs, stories, songs and dances of a particular culture. Folklore is mostly preserved and handed down orally from generation to generation in stories, songs and dances; there is usually the element of embellishment by the various performers of the same dance, song or story over time.

## Folktale

A folktale is a story that has been handed down orally from generation to generation before being written down. Its author is hardly ever known and is accepted generally as a cultural heritage by the culture from which it originates. Such folk narratives as legends, animal tales, trickster stories, fairytales, tall tales and myths fall under the category of folktales.

## Foot

A foot is the basic element in the measurement of a line of metrical poetry. A foot is usually made up of one stressed (') syllable and one or more unstressed syllables ("). The basic known metric feet are the **iamb** (" '), the **spondee** (' '), the **anapaest** (" " '), the **dactyl** (' " '), and the **trochee** (' ").

## Form

Form refers to the structure of a piece of literary work especially a poem.

## Frame Story

This refers to a plot construction that consists of the telling of one story within another story. The story that engulfs the other story and which usually paves the way and follows the inner story is the **frame**. The **inner** story is the most important of the stories told.

## Free Verse

Free verse is poetry that does not follow traditional rules of formal writing with no fixed pattern of meter, rhyme, line length, or stanza arrangement. Most of Odia Ofeimun's poems are written in free verse.

## Genre

A genre is a category or type of literature. The common literary genres are prose fiction and nonfiction), poetry, and drama.

# H–J

## Haiku

It is a traditional Japanese form of poetry that has three lines and seventeen syllables. The first and third are composed of five syllables each while the middle line is made up of seven syllables. A haiku is mostly concerned with nature and is characterized by strong imagery and emotional appeal.

## Hero

A hero is the chief character in a literary piece. His noble deeds and admirable character usually attract the reader's appreciation. In traditional usage, hero applies only to males while heroine applies to females. Today however, hero can be used both for chief male and female characters in a literary work.

## Heroic Couplet

A heroic couplet is a pair of rhymed lines in iambic pentameter.

## Humour

The quality of a literary work of art that makes characters and their conditions seem funny, comical or ridiculous.

## Hyperbole

A hyperbole is a figure of speech that uses exaggeration to express strong emotion, evoke humor or simply make a point. For example when you say, "he has the strength of a whale", you make use of hyperbole.

## Iambic Pentameter

An iambic pentameter is a particular poetic meter with each line comprising of five feet.

## Idiom

An idiom is a saying that takes on a special meaning different from the usual meaning of the words that make it up. For example, "to bell the cat" means to look for trouble.

## Imagery

Imagery refers to writing that evokes an emotional response by means of pictorial language created by writers in a literary work. Writers use sensory details and descriptions to appeal to one of your senses (sight, hearing, smell, touch, taste).

## Internal Rhyme

This refers to rhyme that occurs within a single line of poetry. Meaning can be conveyed and emotions evoked through internal rhyme. In the following line from 'Akmabe, Girl of my Solitude', the internal rhyme is underlined: "<u>Sweet</u> moon, <u>sweet</u> light, <u>sweet</u> purity".

## Irony

Irony refers to a difference, contrast or discrepancy between appearance and reality. There are three forms of irony; situational, verbal and dramatic irony. **Situational irony** exists when someone's expectations are the opposite of the actual outcome of a particular situation. In **Verbal irony**, one thing is said when another is meant. **Dramatic irony** occurs when the audience knows something very important that the characters do not know.

## Juxtaposition

This refers to the placing of two or more distinct things side-by-side in order to compare of contrast them.

# L – N

## Legend

A legend is a traditional story common among people of a given culture which has been handed down from the past. Legends are usually based on actual people and events but tend to become more exaggerated and are full of fantasy as time passes. The Legend of Nakeli wa Embele is common among the Oroko people of Cameroon.

## Literal Language

This is language that is simple, free of embellishment and straight forward. It is the opposite of figurative or literary language, which indirectly express ideas and is usually beautified.

## Local Colour

When a writer makes use of local color, they write in a way that evokes a particular regions pattern of speaking and behaving. Chinua Achebe, Ngugi wa Thiong'o, Nol Alembong and G.D Nyamndi are examples of writers who use the local color of their native lands in their writings.

## Lyric Poetry

This refers to poetry that expresses a speaker's personal thoughts and feelings. Most lyric poetry is usually short and can be sung.

## Magical Realism

This refers to a style of writing in which realistic events, characters, details settings and dialogue are mixed with magical, fantastical and supernatural elements.

## Metaphor

A metaphor is a figure of speech in which two seemingly unlike things are compared or equated. While a simile states a comparison directly, a metaphor implies the comparison, eluding the use of connectives such as *like* or *as*.

## Metonymy

Metonymy refers to the use of one word to stand for another related term. For example *heart* is sometimes used to stand for *mind*.

## Monologue

A monologue refers to a long speech by a character in a literary work.

## Mood

Mood refers to the emotional quality or atmosphere of a literary work. Mood is created by a writer's choice of language, setting, tone, subject matter, sound devices, rhyme and rhythm.

## Motif

A motif is an important or significant idea, phrase, image, description, or detail that is repeated throughout a literary work and that is related to the major theme of the work.

## Motivation

This refers to the stated or implied reason for a character's action in a literary work.

## Myth

A myth is a traditional story usually common among people of a given culture that deals with gods, goddesses, heroes and supernatural forces. A myth sometimes explains a belief, a custom or a force of nature. Myths are different from legends in that they may not have any element of reality in them. Various cultures of the world have myths relating to how the world was made.

## Narrative Poetry

Narrative poetry is verse that tells a story. Traditional poetry such as ballads and epics are examples of narrative poetry.

## Narrator

A narrator is the person who tells a story. The narrator may or may not be a character in the story he/she tells.

## Nonfiction

This refers to factual prose writing about real persons, places or events.

## Novel

A novel is a book-length fictional prose work of art. The novel is more expansive than a short story in terms of plot, setting, character development and themes.

# O&P

**Octave**

An octave refers to the first eight lines of an Italian or Petrarchan sonnet.

**Ode**

An ode is a lyric poem with an elaborate form and structure, expressed in a stately and straight way. Odes could either be intellectual or imaginative.

**Onomatopoeia**

This refers to the use of words or phrases which actually imitate the sound of what they describe.

**Oral Tradition**

This refers to literature handed down from generation to generation by of word of mouth.

**Oxymoron**

This is a figure of speech in which opposites features, qualities etc. are combined. "Hot ice", "frank lie" are all oxymoronic expressions.

**Parable**

A parable is a simple story that points to a moral or religious lesson. Jesus' parable of the sower is used to teach about Christian fruitfulness of faith.

## Paradox

A paradox is a seemingly impossible or contradictory situation or statement which is nevertheless true or possible literally or figuratively.

## Parallelism

This refers to the use of a series of phrases, sentences, or words that have similar grammatical form.

## Parody

This refers to a humorous imitation of another literary work.

## Personification

Personification is a figure of speech that gives an animal, a force of nature or an idea, human qualities or characteristics. For example, we use personification when we say, "he was gripped by the cold hands of death". Here, death is portrayed as having hands like a human being.

## Persuasion

Persuasive writing is usually a non-fiction piece that sets out to influence the reader to think or behave in a particular way. Examples of persuasions are political essays, court appeals, adverts etc. Writers of such non-fiction appeal to logic and emotion, supplication, and marketing techniques to control their readers. The famous Declaration of Independence written by Thomas Jefferson begins with a persuasion.

## Plot

Plot refers to the sequence of events in a fictional narrative or drama. There are various characteristics of the plot. The plot begins with an **exposition** which introduces the characters, setting and a few opening details of the story. The reader's attention is kept by what is referred to as the **narrative hook.** The **conflict** or the problems and complications in the story is brought to a higher level of complication by the **rising action** leading to the **climax**, the point at which the reader gets the highest emotional pitch. The **falling action** logically resolves the climax, leading to the actual **resolution** or **denouement**, which presents the final outcome of the story.

## Poetic License

Poetic license refers to the freedom that poets have to ignore formal or standard rules of grammar or proper diction when they write in order to produce some special effects.

## Poetry

Poetry is a form (genre) of creative or literary expression that emphasizes the line, rather than the sentence as a unit of composition. Poetry is also referred to as verse. Poetry typically uses (but not in all cases) emotional, imaginative language in **metaphors, personification, simile, oxymoron** other figures of speech.

## Point of View

Point of view refers to the relationship that the storyteller or narrator has with the story he or she tells. **First-person point of view** refers to when the story is narrated by one of the characters in the story, referred to as "I". in this case, the reader follows the events in the story from the "I" character's perspective. A story with the **third-person point of view** follows a narrator who reports the thoughts and feelings of one character, referred to as "he" or "she". In a story with an **omniscient** or **all-knowing point of view**, the reader follows a narrator who knows and sees everything about the characters and events; their situation and thoughts (even those they could not reveal themselves).

## Props

This is a term in theatre which refers to the objects and elements of the scenery when a play or movie is put on stage or acted.

## Prose

This refers to writing in which language is not presented in verse (lines). Novels, short stories, treaties and essays are examples of prose.

## Protagonist

A protagonist is the main or central character in a literary work. The main conflict of the story revolves around the protagonist and the reader is meant to sympathize with him/her.

# Q&R

## Quatrain

A quatrain is a poem or stanza with four lines.

## Refrain

A refrain is a line which is repeated regularly in a song or poem.

## Repetition

This refers to the regular recurrence of sounds, words, phrases, lines, stanzas, or sentences in a speech or another piece of writing.

## Resolution

See **plot.**

## Rhetorical Question

A rhetorical question is a question to which no answer is expected. The function of a rhetorical question is to emphasize the obvious answer to the thing which is asked.

## Rhyme

This refers to the repetition of the same stressed vowel sounds and any succeeding sounds in two or more words. There are various types of rhymes, namely; **end rhymes** (which occur at the ends of lines of poetry), **internal rhymes** (which occur within a single line of poetry) and **slant rhymes** (which occur when words include sounds that are similar but are not identical). Slant rhyme may include variations of **consonance** (the repetition of similar consonant sounds) or **assonance** (the repetition of similar vowel sounds).

## Rhyme Scheme

This refers to the pattern that end rhymes form in a stanza or poem. We design the rhyme scheme by assigning a different letter of the alphabet to each new rhyme. Take the following stanza from "Akmabe, Girl of My Erstwhile Dreams" by B.E wa Ngoe

You fill my day with the golden sun a
And train my step the stump to shun a
You shine my rear with a careful stare b
To grace my foe with an assuring glare b
You lead my arm to the green meadow c
To rest; a life you have made mellow c
My weak, little beard you bless with strokes d
To lease the grace that your sweet breath stokes d

## Rhythm

This refers to the pattern of beats created by the arrangement of stressed and unstressed syllables, especially in poetry. The musical quality of poetry is influenced by rhythm. Rhythm can also add emphasis to certain words as well as convey meaning in poetry. Rhythm is either referred to as regular (when the pattern is predictable) or irregular.

**Rising Action**

See plot.

# S

**Sarcasm**

This refers to satire or irony that uses harsh or scathing words to point out limitations or flaws.

**Satire**

Satire refers to that kind of literature which seeks to expose the flaws, shortcomings, follies and ridiculous part of people or societies. George Owel's *Animal Farm* is a satire on the Russian Bolshevik Revolution.

**Scansion**

This refers to the analysis of the meter of a line of poetry. The action is referred to as scanning which involves the noting of stressed and unstressed syllables in a line of verse and the dividing of the lines into its feet or rhythmical units. We mark stressed syllables with (´) and unstressed syllables ( ).

**Scene**

A scene is a subdivision of an act in a play. Each scene typically takes place in a specific setting and time.

**Screenplay**

This refers to a film script which includes the dialogue and the instructions about camera shots and angles.

**Sensory Details**

See imagery.

**Sestet**

This is a six-line stanza or poem.

**Setting**

Setting refers to the time and place in which events in a literary work occur. Setting includes, aside the physical environment, other aspects such as the ideas, values, beliefs and customs of a given place and time.

**Short Story**

A short story is a brief fictional prose narrative usually with a plot, characters, setting, point of view and theme

**Simile**

Simile is a figure of speech which makes use of the words *like* or *as* to make comparison of seemingly unlike things.

## Soliloquy

A soliloquy is a long speech in drama made by a character who is alone on stage. A soliloquy helps the audience understand the private thoughts of a character.

## Sonnet

A sonnet is a lyric poem of fourteen lines, typically written in iambic pentameter. Sonnets usually follow strict patterns of stanza division and rhymes. There are several types of sonnets, namely; **the Shakespearean** or **English sonnet** which consists of three quatrains followed by a couplet. The typical rhyme scheme of this type of sonnet is *abab, cdcd, efef, gg.* The rhyming couplet often settles the issues raised in the preceding quatrains; **the Petrarchan or Italian sonnet** consists of fourteen lines divided into two stanzas, an octave (eight-line stanza) and a sestet (six-line stanza). Usually, the sestet responds to the issues raised in the octave. The typical rhyme scheme of this sonnet is *abbaabba* for the octave and *cdecde* for the sestet.

## Sound Devices

These are techniques used, especially in poetry, to appeal to the ear. These devices are used to enhance rhyme, rhythm and to add music to the poem. Alliteration, assonance, consonance, onomatopoeia etc. are examples of sound devices.

## Speaker

Speaker in poetry refers to the voice that the reader follows similar to the narrator in prose. It should be noted that the speaker could either use the voice of the poet or that of a fictional person or thing. The **tone** and attitude of the speaker towards the subject matter in the poem is highlighted by the speaker's diction (or choice of words).

## Stage Directions

Stage directions are instructions written by a dramatist to describe the appearance and actions of the characters as well as the sets, props, costume and lighting.

## Stanza

A stanza is a group of lines that form a unit in a poem similar to a paragraph in prose.

## Stereotype

A character is said to be a stereotype if he/she/it is not well developed as an individual but represents a collection of traits and mannerisms supposedly shared by all members of a group.

## Stream of Consciousness

This refers to the technique of presenting a character's free flow of emotions, thoughts and memories in a literary work of art.

## Structure

This refers to the particular order or pattern that a writer uses to present ideas. While narratives typically follow a chronological structure, persuasions and expositions may follow varying structure.

## Style

The distinguishing features of expression which are characteristic of an author's writing. These features include choice of words, length and arrangement of sentences as well as the use of figurative language and imagery.

**Surrealist Poetry**

This refers to poetry that expresses the workings of the unconscious mind and how they interact with outer reality. Images from dreams, visions and stream of consciousness are characteristics of this type of poetry.

**Suspense**

This refers to a feeling of anxiety, uncertainty, curiosity and even of fear of what is about to happen next. Suspense is heightened when writers create a situation that presents the protagonist as being in a dangerous position or when his/her life is threatened.

**Symbol**

A symbol is any object, person, place or experience which exists on a literal level but also represents something somewhere else, especially something abstract. For example, in Linus T. Asong's *No Way to Die*, Dennis Nunquam can be said to be a symbol of misery, hopelessness and defeatism.

**Symbolist Poetry**

This is a kind of poetry that emphasizes the expression of suggestions and inward experiences instead of explicit realities.

## Tall Tale

A tall tale is a humorous folklore which contains a lot of exaggerations and invention. Tall tales are common in the American frontier. Tall tale heroes are typically very bold but sometimes seem foolish. They usually are presented to be having supernatural or superhuman abilities or behave as if they do.

## Technical Vocabulary

This refers to words that are unique to a particular art, science, profession, or trade. Technical vocabulary helps emphasize realism.

## Theme

A theme is the central idea or message contained in a literary work that readers can apply to real life. Theme can either be **stated** (articulated directly) or **implied** (revealed gradually through events, dialogue, or description).

## Thesis

The thesis is the central or main idea in a work of non-fiction. Like theme, the thesis can either be **stated** or **implied.**

**Third-person Point of View**

See point of view

**Tone**

Tone refers to a reflection or portrayal of a writer's or speaker's attitude towards the subject matter, as communicated through the choice of words, punctuation, sentence structure and use of figurative language. A variety of attitudes such as sympathy, anger, joy, humor etc. can be conveyed by a writer's or speaker's tone.

**Tragedy**

A tragedy is a play in which the main character suffers downfall. The **tragic hero** is often a dignified or heroic person. The down typically results from outside forces or from a personal weakness such as pride. That weakness is called a **tragic flaw**. Julius Caesar is a celebrated tragic hero in William Shakespeare's historical drama, *Julius Caesar*.

**Triplet**

A triplet is a stanza of three lines, sometimes with an *aaa* rhyme.

**Vernacular**

This refers to the ordinary speech of a particular country or region. Vernacular is the casual form of formal speech. We can describe slang and dialect as forms of vernacular language. Writers use vernacular to employ or enhance realism, especially when their writing is meant to reflect the realities of a particular region or country.

**Verse Paragraph**

A verse paragraph is a group of lines in a poem that forms a unit. A verse paragraph is different from a stanza in that it does not have a fixed number of lines. Many contemporary poems, especially by Africans, have abandoned the stanza tradition and are now written in verse paragraphs.


**Voice**

Voice refers to the distinctive use of language that helps tell of the author's or narrator's identity to the reader. Tone and diction are chief determinants of voice in a literary work.


**Wit**

Wit refers to a show of cleverness and humor in a piece of writing by either the author or a character.

# FURTHER READING


Abrams, M.H. *A Glossary of Literary Terms (7th edition)*. Boston: Heinle and Heinle, 1999.

Bennette, Andrew and Royle, Nicholas. *Introduction to Literature, Criticism and Theory*.3rd Edition. London: Pearson Education Limited, 2004

Burton, R. F. *Wit and Wisdom from West Africa; or, A Book of Proverbial Philosophy, Idioms, Enigmas, and Laconisms*, London, 1965.

Cuddon, J.A. *A Dictionary of Literary Terms and Literary Theory* (5th Edition). The Atrium, Southern Gate, Chichester and Sussex: Wiley-Blackwell, 2013.

Okpewho, Isidore. *Myth in Africa*. London: Cambridge University Press, 1983.

Tyson, Lois. *Critical Theory Today*. New York and London: Routledge Taylor and Francis Group, 2006.

# ABOUT THE AUTHOR

Blessed E. Ngoe comes from Bafaka Balue in the Republic of Cameroon. He is a scholar of Cultural Communication and African Literature with degrees from the University of Buea, Cameroon, and New Mexico State University, USA. Ngoe's research is in cultural communication, the environment, and cultural history. He is the author of the critical treatise, *The Sinking Ship: A Critical Analysis of Multiculturalism in Postcolonial Cameroon*. In 2019, Ngoe founded EboniGram, a digital platform where he publishes a monthly magazine and a news blog about black ideas, black businesses, and black communities.

www.ingramcontent.com/pod-product-compliance
Lightning Source LLC
Chambersburg PA
CBHW051413250726
48655CB00003B/1017